C000176581

Top Tips for CAE

Acknowledgements

Cambridge ESOL is grateful to the following authors and publishers for permission to reproduce copyright material in the text:

The Daily Telegraph for the text on p. 19, adapted from 'Feminism revives the ultra-feminine' by John McEwen, *Sunday Telegraph Review* on 21 April 2002 © Telegraph Group Limited; *The Guardian* for the adapted text on p. 21 adapted from 'Joined up reading' by Harriet Lane, *Observer* on 6 July 2003 © Guardian News & Media.

Every effort has been made to identify the copyright owners for material used, but it has not always been possible to identify the source or contact the copyright holders. In such cases, Cambridge ESOL would welcome information from the copyright owners.

For permission to reproduce photographs:

Imagestate for pictures on page 56.

Cambridge ESOL would also like to thank the following for their contributions to this project:

Sue Elliott, Helen Naylor.

University of Cambridge ESOL Examinations
1 Hills Road, Cambridge, CB1 2EU, UK
www.CambridgeESOL.org

© UCLES 2009
Second printing 2009

First published 2009
Printed in the United Kingdom by Océ (UK) Ltd

ISBN: 978-1-906438-77-7

Contents

Introduction   4

Guide to CAE task types   6

How to revise for CAE   7

Paper 1: Reading   13

Paper 2: Writing   23

Paper 3: Use of English   29

Paper 4: Listening   41

Paper 5: Speaking   51

What to do on the day   64

Computer-based CAE (CB CAE)   68

What next after CAE?   70

Installing the CD-ROM   71

Introduction

Top Tips for CAE is an essential part of your revision for the Certificate in Advanced English (CAE), the C1-level exam from Cambridge ESOL. Each of the five main chapters (Reading, Writing, Use of English, Listening and Speaking) follows the same structure and is based on a series of pieces of advice (the 'tips') which examiners have collected from many years' experience of writing and marking CAE papers.

Each section usually starts with a tip at the top of the page. The tip is followed by an example taken from real CAE material and a clear explanation to help you understand exactly what it means.

Each chapter ends with some more 'General tips' for that paper. There is also a handy section at the beginning of the book on how to revise for CAE and a very important section at the back on what you should do on the day of the exam.

How to use *Top Tips for CAE*

Take the *Top Tips for CAE* book with you and read it when you have a few minutes during the day. Then use the CD-ROM to practise at home: it contains a real CAE exam for you to try, together with the answers for Reading, Use of English and Listening and some sample student answers for the Writing paper. The CD-ROM also includes all the recordings for the Listening paper and a video of real students doing a CAE Speaking test, to show you exactly what you will have to do when you take the test. Practise with some classmates using the Speaking test material on the CD-ROM and compare your performance with the students on the video.

Top Tips for CAE is flexible. You can look at a different tip from a different paper every day, or you can start at the beginning with the tips for the Reading paper and work through until you get to the end of the tips for the Speaking test. Whichever method you prefer, read the example and the explanation carefully to make sure that you understand each tip. When you have understood all the tips for each paper, try the real exam on the CD-ROM.

Guide to symbols

 This symbol introduces the 'tip' which is usually at the top of the page. Each tip is some useful advice to help you find the right answer for Reading, Use of English or Listening. For Writing, the tips show you how to write a better answer to the question, and for Speaking, they explain how you can give good answers which show your true level of English to the examiners.

 This is an extra piece of advice which is important for this particular part of the test.

 This symbol tells you to go to the CD-ROM, where you will find a real CAE exam to try.

We hope that *Top Tips for CAE* will help you with your preparation for taking the CAE exam.

Cambridge ESOL

Guide to CAE task types

Multiple choice You read a text or listen to a recording and then answer questions. Each question has three or four options, only one of which is the correct answer. (*Reading: Parts 1 and 3, Listening: Parts 1 and 3*)

Gapped text You are given a text with some empty spaces. There are some paragraphs after the text, and you have to choose the correct one for each gap. (*Reading: Part 2*)

Multiple matching You read a series of questions and a long text or several short texts or you listen to recordings by different speakers. For each question, you have to decide which text or part of the text, or which speaker mentions this. (*Reading: Part 4, Listening: Part 4*)

Cloze You are given a text with gaps, where words or phrases are missing. There are two types of 'cloze' in the Use of English paper. Part 1 is a multiple-choice cloze task, where you choose from the four options given. Part 2 is an open cloze, where you have to think of the right word for the gap. (*Use of English: Parts 1 and 2*)

Word formation A text containing a number of gaps, with each gap corresponding to a word. A 'prompt' word is given at the end of the line, which you must change to form the missing word. (*Use of English: Part 3*)

Gapped sentences You are given three different sentences for each question. Each sentence contains one gap, and you have to find one word which is appropriate to fill all three gaps. (*Use of English: Part 4*)

Key word transformation A number of sentences, each followed by a key word and a second sentence containing a gap. You have to use the key word to complete the second sentence so that it means the same as the first. You have to use three to six words, one of which must be the key word. (*Use of English: Part 5*)

Sentence completion You listen to a recording of someone speaking, and complete sentences with information you hear on the recording. (*Listening: Part 2*)

Long turn You are given three pictures and you have to talk about two of them for 1 minute without interruption. (*Speaking: Part 2*)

Collaborative task Conversation with the other candidate. The interlocutor gives you some pictures and a decision-making task to do. You have to talk with the other candidate and make a decision. (*Speaking: Part 3*)

How to revise for CAE

It is important to use, as well as possible, the time that you have to revise for CAE. Here are some general ideas to help you do this.

Make a plan

It is a good idea to make a plan for your last month's study before the exam. Think about:

- what you need to do
- how much time you have
- how you can fit what you need to do into that time.

Try to be realistic when you make your plan. If you plan to do too much, then you may soon be disappointed when you fall behind.

Think about what you need to know

Remember that CAE is a test of your general level of English. You don't have an exam syllabus listing what information you have to learn as you do in, for example, chemistry or history. So most things that you do in English will help you to improve – reading a story or a newspaper article or listening to an English radio programme may be as useful as doing a grammar exercise, for example.

It is important, however, that you know exactly what you will have to do in the exam. Doing some practice papers will help you develop good exam techniques and this will save you time in the exam room. But don't spend all your revision time doing practice papers!

Think about what you need to improve. Ask your English teacher what you need to work on – reading, writing, listening, or speaking, or how English is used.

Look back at homework that your teacher has corrected. What mistakes did you make? Do you understand where you went wrong? What are your weaknesses?

Have what you need to hand

In order to prepare for CAE you probably need:

- a good learners' dictionary (one with examples of how words are actually used in English)
- a bilingual dictionary
- a good grammar book
- a CAE-level coursebook (you are probably using one of these if you do regular classes)
- some examples of CAE papers
- a vocabulary notebook
- notes or other materials from your English course (if you are doing one).

If you have access to a computer you can get some of these online – the dictionaries and the examples of CAE papers, for instance.

Also have a good supply of stationery such as pens, pencils, highlighters and paper. Some students find it convenient to write things like vocabulary on cards, which they then carry with them and look at when they have a spare moment on the bus or in a café.

Think about when and where you study

Most people find it best to study at regular times at a desk with a good light and everything they need beside them.

Some people find they work best in the early mornings while others prefer the evenings. If possible, do most of your revision at the time of day which is best for you.

You may also find that there are other good times and places for you to study. Perhaps when you are making a meal or doing some housework you could listen to some English on an mp3 player. Or you could read something on your way to work or school.

Organise your revision time well

Allow time for breaks when you are revising – many students like to study for an hour and a half, for example, and then have a half-hour break.

Vary what you do – sometimes focus on listening, sometimes on vocabulary, sometimes on writing. This will make sure that you don't neglect any aspect of the language and will also make your revision more interesting.

It is sensible to do something completely different before you go to bed – go for a walk, read a relaxing book or watch a favourite film.

Enjoy your revision!

Find some enjoyable activities that help your English – listen to songs in English or watch TV or some English-language DVDs.

What do you like doing in your free time? Could you combine that with English practice too? For example, if you like a particular sport or singer, or if you are interested in computer games, you should easily be able to find something in English about your interest on the internet.

Revise with a friend – you can practise talking to each other in English and can perhaps help each other with any questions you have.

Keep fit!

Don't forget that feeling fit and healthy will help you get good marks too:

* make sure you get enough sleep
* remember to eat well
* take some exercise.

Now here are some ideas to help you organise your revision for the individual papers in CAE.

Paper 1: Reading

The more you read in English before the exam, the better you will do in this paper. Reading is probably the best way to improve your grammar and vocabulary.

You will learn most if you enjoy what you are reading. So don't choose something that is too difficult for you. Remember that it doesn't have to be serious – unless, of course, you prefer serious things. There are lots of different students who enjoy each of these types of reading:

- newspaper articles
- sports magazines
- film reviews
- romantic stories
- children's stories
- travel information – about your own country or a place you have been to
- translations of books you have already read in your own language
- graded readers (well-known books which are adapted to your level of English).

Don't look up every word in a dictionary when you read as this will spoil your pleasure in reading. Just look up anything that is essential for understanding. Then when you have finished you can go back and look up some more words and make a note of any useful expressions from the text.

Keep a reading diary – write a couple of sentences in English about what you have read. This should help you to use some of the language from what you have read. It will also help you with the Writing paper.

Paper 2: Writing

For this paper, it is important to practise writing regularly in English.

- Use some of the new vocabulary and expressions that you have learned from your reading.

- If possible ask a teacher or native English speaker to correct your work. Ask them to correct your mistakes and also to suggest a more interesting way of expressing what you want to say.
- Listen carefully to their advice and use it in the next piece of writing that you do.

Paper 3: Use of English

This is the paper where doing practice tests may help you most. However, you also need to have a good control of grammar and vocabulary to do well.

- Do some extra practice with materials which focus on grammar and vocabulary (your teacher may be able to advise you which books are best).
- Research shows that you learn best when you write or talk about things that are important to you. So practise making sentences about your own life and experience using structures or vocabulary that you want to learn.
- When you read or listen to English, think about the language that the writer or speaker is using and pay attention to the way that they combine words.

Paper 4: Listening

Even if you are a long way from an English-speaking country, it is possible to practise listening to English. For example, there are lots of things you can listen to on television, the radio or the internet.

- Listen to short programmes in English on the radio or on an English-language TV channel as much as possible.
- Watch DVDs of English-language films. You may be able to watch a film with subtitles. This can make listening easier and more enjoyable and will help to give you confidence in listening to English.
- Try watching a film in English that you have already seen in your own language.
- Listening to songs in English can be an enjoyable and relaxing way of listening to English. It is often possible to find the words for songs on the internet.

Paper 5: Speaking

Make the effort to practise speaking English whenever you can.

- Get together with friends and agree that you will speak only English for half an hour.
- Join an English-language club if there is one in your area.
- Try to make contact with English speakers visiting your area. Perhaps you could get some work as a tour guide.
- If there are students whose first language is English in your area, try to arrange to exchange conversation sessions with them. (You talk for half an hour in your language and half an hour in English.)
- When listening to English-language films or television, think about the language that the speakers use and, where possible, make use of it when you are speaking yourself.
- Make sure that you can talk about yourself, give opinions, ask someone to repeat or explain, agree and disagree. You may need to do all of these things in the exam.

We hope these ideas will help you to make the most of your revision time. Above all, we hope that you enjoy your studies and wish you all the very best for the exam.

Paper 1: Reading

What's in the Reading paper?

Part 1 ⓠ 3 texts on the same theme. Each text is followed by 2 multiple-choice questions
☑ 2 marks for each correct answer

Part 2 ⓠ gapped text with 6 paragraphs removed
☑ 2 marks for each correct answer

Part 3 ⓠ text with 7 multiple-choice questions
☑ 2 marks for each correct answer

Part 4 ⓠ 1 long text or several shorter texts with 15 multiple-matching questions
☑ 1 mark for each correct answer

🕐 **1 hour 15 minutes**

Reading: Part 1 multiple choice

 TIP: You won't always be asked to find the answer to a complete question. You may instead be asked to choose the best option to complete a sentence about the text.

Example

Here is an extract from a Part 1 text about companies developing new products, and one of the questions.

> Businesses nowadays are faced with bigger problems than ever before. For a relatively low cost, consumers can have all the technological and aesthetic features they want on their products. This has made it difficult for companies to differentiate themselves on product features in the way they used to. They need to produce something that no one else has, or has even thought of, and which others cannot copy because of its patent, its legal protection.

 The reason the writer gives for the difficulties experienced by many companies is that

    A their products are sold too cheaply.

    B their customers are not loyal to their products.

    C their products possess no unique advantage.

    D their products are copied by rival businesses.

Explanation: The highlighted words in the text show that **C** is the answer. It's important to remember the beginning of the sentence (e.g. 'The reason the writer gives . . .') as you look through each of the four options.

Reading: Part 1 multiple choice

 TIP: Some questions may focus on the opinions, attitudes and feelings that are being expressed, so it's important to practise reading texts which help you to recognise these.

Example

Here is an extract from a Part 1 text about developing products, and one of the questions.

I recently visited an inventors' exhibition. There they were, ploughing their own specialist furrows, living in hope that someone might approach them and like their ideas. Not to put too fine a point on it, the exhibitors looked and sounded like a bunch of amateurs. What a waste of effort! Even if they had come up with a good idea, they would be more than likely to find that industry was not interested, quite simply because the timing was wrong. In other words, there was very little market awareness deployed in the process.

 When visiting the inventors' exhibition, the writer felt

A bored by the event.

B sympathetic to the exhibition organisers.

C discouraged by what he saw.

D optimistic about the future.

Explanation: The highlighted words in the text indicate that C is the answer, but the tone of the whole paragraph expresses a negative attitude.

Reading: Part 2 gapped text

TIP: Look for clues that indicate there is a link between the paragraph that you think is the answer, and the paragraphs before and after it. This will involve reading more carefully than just matching similar words and phrases.

Example

Here is an extract from a Part 2 text about climbing in Spain.

'You're going up there, without crampons and an ice axe?' asked the farmer incredulously. He was pointing to the upper reaches of the 3,300 m Sierra Nevada, the highest peaks in the Spanish mainland. I shrugged. I had my trekking pole. And after the previous day's snowstorm, the sky was a faultless blue. It looked like a perfect summit day.

> I kicked at the ground. Eighty centimetres of snow had fallen during the previous twenty-four hours. 'Well, at least the slope isn't slippery,' I retorted.

The farmer raised his face to the sun. 'Not yet, but it's still early.' It was. As the sun rose, my eyes narrowed into slits. There was a dull throb behind my eyes. 'I should have brought sunglasses,' I mumbled. Then I left both farmer and the tree line behind and began my ascent.

Explanation: The missing paragraph is inserted in the text. The word 'retorted' shows that the speaker is responding to someone else, possibly offering a contrasting view. In the rest of the text, the speaker has no other contact with people, which further confirms that the paragraph is correct. The next part confirms the choice of paragraph – the farmer says 'Not yet' suggesting that something (the sun) might change the conditions of the slope.

Remember there is always one extra paragraph in Part 2 which does not fit anywhere in the text.

Reading: Part 2 gapped text

 TIP: If you are not sure which is the correct paragraph to fit in the gap, try eliminating the ones you haven't used so far.

Example

Here is an extract from a Part 2 text about climbing in Spain.

> Before I knew what was happening, one foot failed to gain a hold. My water bottles ripped free of the rucksack and tumbled downwards before disappearing. I lay motionless, trying to regain control of my thoughts.
>
> > When I had finally calmed down, it became obvious to me, as it would have to anyone with real mountain experience, that it was madness to try and reach the peak.
>
> So instead I began to descend slowly ...

Explanation: The missing paragraph is inserted in the text. The highlighted words show the links across paragraphs which indicate that this paragraph is the correct answer. Look at the beginnings of the other paragraphs from the task to see why they were not suitable:

- *Finally, disorientated by all this, I lay still.* 'I lay still' is unnecessary repetition of 'I lay motionless' in the previous paragraph.
- *I rolled sideways as I fell. Several metres passed.* This does not fit the order of events, as the speaker has already fallen and landed, lying 'motionless', in the previous paragraph.
- *Yet every step took me further from my rational mind. I went up rapidly ...* In the previous paragraph the speaker was 'motionless', and in the one after he was descending, not ascending.

Reading: Part 3 multiple choice

 TIP: In multiple-choice questions the option you choose must always be supported by information in the text. You may find it useful to underline the part of the text containing the answer, to check you are correct.

Example

Here is an extract from a Part 3 text about inventions, with one of the questions.

> As with any other area of business, you need to start with a clear brief. It could be streamlining a food processor or re-branding a service; there is the outline of the client's demands, the thought and development process and finally a solution. For instance, one of the country's leading bicycle manufacturers wanted to improve sales of its brake blocks. Cyclists were not replacing them because they did not know when they were worn out. <u>We managed to devise the world's first brake block that signalled when it was wearing out</u>. My company delivered on paper the final design in just four weeks from the original business request. The product soon became the country's number one brake block, far outstripping sales by competitors.

 Why was the brake block designed by the writer's company so successful?

   A It was such a straightforward design.

   B It wore out less quickly than the others.

   C It performed more effectively than others.

   D It was obvious when it needed replacing. ✓

Explanation: The part which gives the answer is underlined in the text.

Reading: Part 3 multiple choice

 TIP: If you are not sure which of the four options is correct, try a process of elimination. This can take longer, but if you are stuck, it may help you get the answer.

Example

Here is an extract from a Part 3 text about the 19th century painter, Berthe Morisot, with one of the questions.

> On her honeymoon in 1875, the French Impressionist painter Berthe Morisot wrote, 'There is extraordinary life and movement, but how is one to render it?' That she managed is abundantly proved by the current Berthe Morisot (1841–95) exhibition in Lille, France, the first major show of her work for 40 years. It opens with three paintings from the late 1860s which, although they do not exhibit the scintillating sketchiness of her mature style, certainly establish the youthful and domestic focus which so characterises her work – no men, no older people to spoil the youthful idyll, but young women enjoying the homely comforts of ordinary life.

 What does the writer say about the three pictures at the start of the Berthe Morisot exhibition?

A They have a wide and varied subject matter.

B They reflect Morisot's struggle to capture lively scenes.

C They introduce us to recurring themes in Morisot's art. ✓

D They are painted in a style that Morisot returned to in later years.

Explanation: The highlighted parts of the text show where the answer can be found.

A is incorrect, as the paintings had a domestic focus only – 'no men, no older people ... but young women ...' ✗

B is incorrect, as she portrayed 'the homely comforts of ordinary life'. ✗

D is incorrect as the paintings 'do not exhibit the scintillating sketchiness of her mature style'. ✗

 *Don't be put off by vocabulary you don't know, such as 'scintillating sketchiness' in this text. Continue reading the text to see if the meaning becomes clear.*

Reading: Part 4 multiple matching

 TIP: Underline key words in the questions as this is helpful when trying to locate the information in the text that provides the answers.

Example

Here is one of the extracts from a Part 4 task, a review of a book, together with three statements which match the text.

> **Q** **Which review mentions the following?**
>
> **1** some stories which depart somewhat unsuccessfully from Proulx's usual themes
>
> **4** a concise style of writing that is very effective
>
> **9** the book being worth reading despite not having the same force as Proulx's previous one

> **A** These are some of Annie Proulx's best stories. The book falls down, though, with the inclusion of a handful of stories that veer into magical realism. These flights of fantasy sit uneasily with those grounded in the dry earth, sagebrush and fierce sunlight – the very soul of a Wyoming that Annie Proulx's writing is so at home in. As a result, *Bad Dirt* makes a lesser impression than *Close Range*, her earlier collection of stories about Wyoming. Even so, great pleasure is still to be had from Annie Proulx's singular style of writing. She has a masterful ability to condense a character's life into punchy sentences that underpin vivid images. It is this creativeness, coupled with a powerful sense of place, that makes *Bad Dirt* a good read.

> **1**
> **1**
> **1**
> **9**
>
> **9**
>
> **4**

Explanation: The highlighted sections show a match for the key words underlined in questions 1, 4 and 9. You may find it useful in the exam to highlight or underline where you think the answer comes from as well as the key words in the questions.

Reading: Part 4 multiple matching

TIP: There may be information in the text that looks very similar to what is in the options, but it may not be close enough to be a good match. Read carefully around where you think the answer comes from to make sure you are correct.

Example

Here is an extract from a Part 4 text about book clubs, with some questions. Some of the questions don't match this extract.

> (Q) **1** Which group member attended a group which originally also dealt with other branches of the arts? ✓
>
> **2** Which group member set up a group for the benefit of another person?
>
> **3** Which group member attended a group where catering was a matter of pride?

A Sue Field

Thirty-seven years ago – decades before reading groups became popular – three British women began talking in the maternity unit of a hospital. After returning home, they kept in touch and began to meet socially with five other members from the area. 'We were all in the same boat, with our first babies, wanting to get away from child talk sometimes and engage our brains, challenge our minds, if you like,' says Sue. Group members took it in turns to host the evening, providing a 'bought, not made' pudding (there was a main course originally, but it was dropped – too much hassle). Initially, classical records were played, and reproductions of paintings discussed, but the books soon elbowed out the competition, so it became a reading group.

2

3
1

Explanation:

1 This matches the extract. ✓

2 The group was not for one person, but several. ✗

3 Catering is mentioned, but it is not a source of pride – they buy their puddings rather than make them, and abandon the main course as it is 'too much hassle'. ✗

General tips for Reading

1 When preparing for the test, try to read as widely as you can, from as many different text types as possible.

2 Try to interact with the text and form an opinion about what you're reading.

3 Read each question at least twice before you attempt it.

4 Check that the answer you've chosen reflects all parts of the question.

5 In **Part 2**, read the whole text and all the missing paragraphs before you start to decide which paragraph fits in which part of the text.

6 Don't spend too much time on any one part of the paper.

7 Leave time to check your answers to challenging questions.

 NOW YOU TRY! You will find Reading Parts 1, 2, 3 and 4 to try on the CD-ROM. Give yourself 1 hour 15 minutes to work through the whole paper.

When you have finished you can check your answers.

Paper 2: Writing

What's in the Writing paper?

Part 1 ⓠ 1 compulsory question (180–220 words)
You read some material (up to 150 words) –
advertisements, extracts from letters, emails,
postcards, diaries, short articles, etc. Then you write
an article, a report, a proposal or a letter using the
information in the material

Part 2 ⓠ 1 question from a choice of 5 (220–260 words)
including an article, a competition entry, a contribution
to a longer piece, an essay, an information sheet, a
letter, a proposal, a report, a review

 each question carries equal marks

 1 hour 30 minutes

Your writing is assessed first of all for content – have you covered all
the points in the task? It is then assessed for the following:

- the organisation and cohesion of your writing
- the range of language you have used
- the accuracy of your language
- the register and tone you have selected – formal, informal or neutral
- the format – have you chosen the right layout for the task,
  e.g. report, review, etc?
- the word length of your writing – is it too short? or much too long?
- your overall effectiveness in dealing with the tasks.

Writing: **Part 1**

 TIP: You should make an early reference to why you're writing – make sure you've included an appropriate introduction. Ask yourself who you are writing to and why.

Example

Here is an example of a Part 1 task.

You have been working as a Student Adviser at a Language Academy in your country, but you will finish next month. Your English friend, Sam, is coming to study in your country, and wants to earn some money while there. You decide to write a letter to Sam about the job.

Using the information in the job description below, write a letter to Sam, describing the job, suggesting why Sam should apply and explaining how to deal with any of the problems.

> **Midtown Language Academy requires**
> **Part-time Student Adviser**
> - minimum 8 weeks
> - organise events
> - deal with student problems
> Benefits
> - free shared accommodation
> - paid weekly
> - flexible hours

lots to do, e.g. ... (get help)

my house better because ...

Explanation: In this question, you might start as follows:

> Hi Sam,
> Hope you're well. How's life in England? Thought
> I'd drop you a line as I understand you're planning
> to come to my country soon to study, and you'll be
> looking for a job.
> Well, I may have the perfect solution for you! . . .

Make sure you include all the information you've been asked for in the question and the notes.

Writing: **Part 1**

 TIP: Make sure you allow enough time to proofread (check) your work before the end of the exam. That's important – it's easy to make basic slips when you're writing to a time limit.

Example

Look at the following example. It includes mistakes which have been underlined.

> There's not need to worry about acommodation. I can put up you at my home, no problem. It'd be a pleasures to have you to stay.

Here is the corrected version.

> There's no need to worry about accommodation. I can put you up at my home, no problem. It'd be a pleasure to have you to stay.

Use this checklist to help you to proofread your writing.

Checklist	✔
Have you addressed the right person in your answer?	
Have you included all the points in your answer?	
Is your piece of writing the right length?	
Have you started and finished your answer appropriately?	
Is your answer in the appropriate style, i.e. formal, informal or neutral?	
Have you written in the appropriate register?	
Have you proofread your answer for grammar and spelling mistakes?	
Have you used a varied range of grammar and vocabulary, or have you relied on a limited range?	
Have you used suitable linking words to connect your ideas?	
Have you used a suitable layout (e.g. leaflet, report)? Do you need subheadings? Is it paragraphed correctly?	
Would your piece of writing be successful in real life? Would it get the response you hope for?	

Writing: Part 2

 TIP: Make sure your answer relates to the question, rather than being too general.

Example

Here is an example of a Part 2 task.

> **You have been asked to provide a personal reference for a friend who has applied for a job as a personal assistant to an international film star. The job involves making travel arrangements, attending important social events and dealing with the media. The reference should:**
>
> - **say how long you have known your friend**
> - **describe the skills and experience that your friend would bring to the job**
> - **explain why your friend would be the best person for the job.**

Here is the second part of a sample answer.

Paul has worked extensively in the entertainment sector, most recently as a very competent PA to a pop star, so he is very familiar with this environment.	has experience in the field
His job required good organisational and communication skills and the need to think on his feet, which he proved very good at.	likely to be useful in the new job
He is skilled in the use of IT and has the ability to remain calm in a crisis. He is also trustworthy,	best person for the job not just a good person
always punctual and dedicated to his work. I believe he would bring all of these to the	skills related to the job
new job.	

Explanation: Writing a reference may require a certain amount of work-related vocabulary, and the answer **must** relate to the job specified in the question, as it does here.

Writing: Part 2

 TIP: Make sure you practise writing different text types such as letters, reports, proposals and articles. Check that you know the conventions for writing these.

Example

Here is an example of a Part 2 task.

> **You see this announcement on your mobile phone company's website.**
>
> As you use our services, we want to hear what *you* think. How has having a mobile affected the way you work or socialise? Also, give us an example of a time when having a mobile really helped you, and say what might have happened if you hadn't had one.
>
> Send us your article. The best ones will appear on this website, and win you a year of free calls!

Explanation: Look at the sample answer below.

> Dear Sir or Madam,
> I am writing in reply to your announcement on your company website.
> I am pleased to tell you that having a phone from your company has helped me many times both in work and social situations ...

This reply is in the form of a letter rather than an article, and is addressed to the wrong target audience – the mobile phone company rather than readers of the website.

Compare it with this sample answer.

> MY MOBILE - CAN'T LIVE WITHOUT IT!
> I simply can't remember a time when I didn't have a mobile phone! How on earth did I manage? I rely on it completely these days to arrange my social life - in fact if I didn't have a phone, I'd probably never get to meet up with friends!

General tips for Writing

1 Writing is the same as any other skill – it's impossible to master it without practising. Try to write regularly in English. Think about who you are writing to, why you are writing, and what sort of text it should be.

2 Build your vocabulary as much as you can – reading widely can help with this. You might also try learning a range of words in different categories, e.g. work-related words, words to do with travelling. Learning whole expressions that you can use in your writing can also be very useful.

3 Make sure you can use a range of tenses accurately and appropriately.

4 Before you start writing, spend a few minutes planning what you are going to say. Make sure you are going to answer the question, rather than writing something irrelevant or too general – there isn't time for this in the exam.

5 Check your work. Do you have any particular mistakes that you always tend to make, e.g. leaving out articles? Be aware of the typical mistakes you tend to make and check your work carefully for them.

6 In **Part 1**, check you have included all the information you've been asked to.

7 In **Part 2**, make sure you select the question that you can write about most comfortably.

 NOW YOU TRY! You will find Writing Parts 1 and 2 to try on the CD-ROM. Give yourself 1 hour 30 minutes to work through the whole paper.

When you have finished you can compare your answers to the sample answers.

Paper 3: Use of English

What's in the Use of English paper?

Part 1 ⓠ text with 12 gaps and 4 multiple-choice options for each gap
☑ 1 mark for each correct answer

Part 2 ⓠ text with 15 gaps
☑ 1 mark for each correct answer

Part 3 ⓠ text with 10 gaps and the stems of missing words. You change the word to fit the gap
☑ 1 mark for each correct answer

Part 4 ⓠ 5 questions, each containing 3 separate sentences with a gap. You write a word that fits all 3 sentences
☑ 2 marks for each correct answer

Part 5 ⓠ 8 separate sentences. Each sentence is followed by a keyword and a second sentence with a gap. You complete the second sentence using 3–6 words, one of which is the key word
☑ up to 2 marks for each correct answer

🕐 **1 hour**

Use of English: Part 1 multiple-choice cloze

 TIP: Read the whole text to make sure you know what it is about and that you understand the context.

Examples

Here are some examples of the different grammar and vocabulary points which can be tested in Part 1.

1 The four options may be similar in meaning but the surrounding context will determine which one is correct. Here is an example from a text about Swiss railways.

The public system has 3,000 kilometres of some of the most spectacular _____ in Europe.

A paths   **B** routes ✓   **C** courses   **D** trails

Explanation: The text is about Swiss railways, and 'routes' is the only appropriate word for a transport system.

2 Some questions may ask you to choose between different phrasal verbs.

At the points where the trains stop, yellow buses or lake steamers _____ – all on the same ticket.

A go across   **B** take over ✓   **C** fill in   **D** keep on

Explanation: A phrasal verb is needed that has the sense of 'replace' or 'take their place' – so 'take over' is the most suitable choice.

3   In some questions, the grammatical context determines which
    option is correct, for example when considering which option
    will fit with the preposition that precedes or follows it. Here is an
    example from a text about the rise of aviation.

If people did not have the natural ability to fly which they
_____ for, they certainly had no lack of ingenuity and ideas.

A dreamed   B envied   C aspired   D longed ✓

Explanation: Of the four options, only 'longed' can be followed by
the preposition 'for'.

4   Some questions can test your knowledge of set phrases. Here is
    an example from a text about the problems of tourism.

Complaints about the impact of tourist numbers were being
made when tourism, in the modern _____ , hardly existed.

A concept   B significance   C term   D sense ✓

Explanation: This requires the completion of a set phrase: 'in the
modern sense' is a set phrase.

Use of English: Part 2 open cloze

TIP: Read the whole text and then read carefully around the gap to see what kind of word is required, e.g. noun, verb, linking word.

Examples

Here are some examples of the different kinds of words that can be tested in Part 2. They are taken from two texts about light pollution and killer whales. The correct answers are in the gaps for you.

1 Relative pronouns

> The main cause of light pollution in the UK is five million street lights, most of ...**which**... are left on all night.

2 Phrasal verbs

> It was pointed ...**out**... that street lights can waste money and cause environmental pollution.

3 Conjunctions

> ...**Although**... these lamps are more expensive, just four are needed for every five of the old type.

4 Prepositions

> The problem was brought ...**to**... the attention of the public in 1990.

5 Verbs

> Some populations of killer whales have declined over the past 30 years, which ...**is**... exactly the same period that has seen a decrease in prey species.

6 Set phrases

> When one calf mounted an attack, its mother stayed in ...**close**... contact all the time.

Other words tested include articles, auxiliaries, pronouns, verb tenses and forms.

Use of English: **Part 2** open cloze

 TIP: Sometimes you may need to read a large chunk of text to see which word is required – reading what goes before and after the gap will not be enough to give you the answer.

Examples

1   It may be necessary to complete a **structure**, the two parts of which are separated in the text.

> 'Fully-shielded lights **not** ...**only**... help preserve the beauty of the starry sky,' maintains David Crawford of the International Dark Skies Association, 'but they also illuminate far more efficiently.'

Explanation: The missing word is 'only', as it is part of the structure 'not only ... but also', which is spread across the chunk of text.

2   It is important to read and understand the text before the gap in order to select a word with the correct **meaning**.

> Researchers found that identical twins, who share the same genes, tended to have the same levels of musical ability. ...**However**... , non-identical twins, who share just 50% of the same genes were less likely to have the same level of musical talent.

Explanation: From reading the chunk of text, it becomes clear that a link is needed that contrasts the abilities of the identical and non-identical twins.

Use of English: Part 3 word formation

 TIP: There will be different kinds of changes you need to make to the words at the end of the line. Look carefully to see what kind of word is needed and then think about the form required.

Example

Here is an example from a Part 3 text about penguins. The correct answers have been put in the gaps for you.

> The emperor penguin feeds ❶<u>exclusively</u> at sea, diving to ❷<u>depths</u> of 265 metres, and can stay underwater for 18 minutes. It has developed an ❸<u>exceptional</u> talent for surviving in Antarctica, one of the world's harshest environments. The penguin has ❹<u>unusually</u> thick plumage which keeps it warm, and its flippers and legs are specially adapted to minimise heat loss.
>
> ① EXCLUSIVE
> ② DEEP
>
> ③ EXCEPT
>
> ④ USUAL

Explanation: You may need to:

*   add a suffix to the end of the word
    e.g. EXCLUSIVE becomes exclusively

*   make a change to the spelling of the word; (you may also need to make a word plural)
    e.g. DEEP becomes depths

*   add more than one prefix or suffix
    e.g. EXCEPT becomes exceptional

*   add a prefix to the beginning and a suffix to the end of the word
    e.g. USUAL becomes unusually.

You must make sure in each case that the **spelling** is correct.

Use of English: **Part 3** word formation

 TIP: You should read the whole text carefully first to see what it is about, and to make it easier to see what kind of word is missing. The context may determine that the missing word is, for example a negative or a plural. Read each full sentence (not just the line) before deciding on your answer.

Example

Here is an example from a Part 3 text about vitamins. The correct answers have been put in the gaps for you.

We know there are large ❶<u>variations</u> in each person's vitamin requirements, so we at *Healthcare* have created a range of great vitamin supplements to match your nutritional needs. These ❷<u>outstanding</u> products are only available by post, and we're offering them to our customers at ❸<u>unbeatable</u> prices.	① VARY ② STAND ③ BEAT

Explanation: We know that ① must be plural to match the preceding verb 'are'. The text is clearly promotional, for a company called *Healthcare,* and this helps in deciding which form of the given word you need in ② and ③, as both adjectives have to be extremely positive. This gives 'outstanding' in ② – meaning excellent, above the rest – and 'unbeatable' in ③ – meaning that it can't be improved because of its excellent quality.

 *The form of the word you are looking for may be determined by the context of the whole text, not just the immediate context of the language preceding and following the gap.*

Use of English: Part 4 gapped sentences

 TIP: Decide what kind of word is needed. For example, is it a verb, a noun or an adjective? The missing word must make sense and be grammatically correct in all three sentences. It may not necessarily be the same part of speech.

Examples

Here are some sentences from a Part 4 task.

> I respect your opinion and will _____ you whatever decision you make.
>
> So many people came to see the procession that those at the _____ of the crowd couldn't see much.
>
> A train is coming so please stand _____ from the edge of the platform.

Explanation: The missing word is **back** (used as a verb, a noun and an adverb), which fits in all three of the sentences.

> Rosa has asked us to _____ the stamps on all the post we get.
>
> If you're late, we'll _____ you a place at our table.
>
> Fernando served so well he was able to _____ the match.

Explanation: The missing word is the verb **save,** which fits in all three of the sentences.

Use of English: Part 4 gapped sentences

 TIP: Read all three sentences and see if you can find a word that fits one of the gaps. Think of other meanings that might be associated with that word. Then check to see if it fits the other gaps too. Make sure the word you choose fits in all three sentences.

Examples

Here are some sentences from a Part 4 task.

James flew from Australia to London and _____ the journey for a few days in Singapore.

My father was fined quite a lot of money because he _____ the 100 km speed limit on the motorway.

It was when I was playing basketball that I fell and _____ my arm.

Explanation: The missing word is **broke,** which fits in all three of the sentences.

Karl was irritated because he couldn't see the _____ of doing that particular job.

From a practical _____ of view, their current house is much too small for them all.

Do you know what the boiling _____ of water is?

Explanation: The missing word in the three sentences is **point**.

 *If you are really stuck, think what **kind** of word is needed in the gaps.*

Use of English: Part 5 key word transformations

TIP: Remember that there is always more than one point being tested, so decide what kind of additional language you need to complete the second sentence. You must not change the key word in any way.

Examples

Here are some examples (with answers) from Part 5.

---

1 This bag is so heavy that I can only just lift it into the car.
ANY
If this bag was ... **any heavier I wouldn't** ... be able to lift it into the car.

Explanation: comparative + conditional clause

---

2 John said he was coming to the cinema with us this evening but it seems he has decided not to.
CHANGED
John appears ... **to have changed his mind about** ... coming to the cinema with us this evening.

Explanation: perfect infinitive + synonymous phrase

---

3 The historian wore gloves so that the fragile documents he was studying would not be damaged.
AVOID
The historian wore gloves ... **to avoid damaging** ... the fragile documents he was studying.

Explanation: infinitive + gerund

---

4 When Billy went to Tenerife, he wished he had learnt some Spanish beforehand.
REGRETTED
When he went to Tenerife, Billy ... **regretted not having learnt** ... some Spanish beforehand.

Explanation: negative + perfect participle

Use of English: **Part 5** key word transformations

 TIP: You should only use 3–6 words to fill the gap. If you add more words, you will lose marks. Don't add any words that are not necessary.

Examples

Here are some examples (with answers) of Part 5 questions.

---

1 It hasn't snowed quite as much this year as last year.
SLIGHTLY
This year, it has snowed … **slightly less than it** … did last year. ✓

---

2 Despite being in his nineties Mr Archer is absolutely determined to carry on driving.
INTENTION
Mr Archer … **hasn't any intention at all of giving** … up driving, despite being in his nineties. ✗

Explanation: If you remove 'at all', the sentence would get full marks.

---

3 As soon as I turned my mobile on it started to ring.
JUST
I … **had just turned my new mobile on** … when it started to ring. ✗

Explanation: If you remove 'new' this sentence would be correct.

 *Contractions count as two words, apart from 'can't', which can be written as one word (cannot).*

General tips for Use of English

1 Think about different ways of learning vocabulary, for example reading widely. See which learning strategies suit you best.

2 It's important to build your knowledge of areas like set phrases, dependent prepositions and phrasal verbs.

3 Practise the different forms of new words you come across (noun, verb, adjective, adverb) and any collocations. Keep a record of them.

4 Look carefully at the titles of texts as they will help you understand what the main theme is.

5 In the exam, plan your time carefully so that you don't spend too much time on any one part.

6 Check your spelling carefully. You will not get a mark if the spelling is incorrect.

7 Read the instructions and examples on all parts of the paper carefully to make sure you know what kind of answers you are expected to give and how to show your answers on the answer sheet.

8 Make sure your handwriting is clear and easy to understand. The answers to **Parts 2, 3, 4** and **5** must be in capital letters.

 NOW YOU TRY! You will find a complete Use of English paper to try on the CD-ROM. Give yourself 1 hour to work through the whole paper.

When you have finished you can check your answers.

Paper 4: Listening

What's in the Listening paper?

Part 1 Ⓠ 3 short texts with 2 multiple-choice questions on each text
☑ 1 mark for each correct answer

Part 2 Ⓠ a longer listening text with 8 sentence-completion questions
☑ 1 mark for each correct answer

Part 3 Ⓠ a longer listening text with 6 multiple-choice questions
☑ 1 mark for each correct answer

Part 4 Ⓠ 5 short themed monologues with 10 multiple-matching questions
☑ 1 mark for each correct answer

🕐 Approximately **40 minutes**
(including 5 minutes to copy your answers onto the answer sheet)

Listening: Part 1 multiple choice

 TIP: When deciding which of the three multiple-choice options is correct, try to identify where the speaker answers the question.

Example

Here is a question from a Part 1 task about youth hostels, together with part of the tapescript.

 In the woman's opinion, recent changes in youth hostels are due to people's desire to

   A stay in cities rather than the countryside.

   B use their cars when they're on holiday.

   C enjoy improved accommodation. ✓

TAPESCRIPT

MAN: *In my day, youth hostelling was about a cheap place to stay – for walkers, in the country. Why've they ruined it all?*

WOMAN: *I don't think they have. The idea is the same as ever – meeting new people, discovering new places. The whole experience isn't really made very different just because you turn up in a car. It's just that people's expectations have shifted – they're not so prepared to rough it these days. There are youth hostels in cities now certainly, but the vast majority are still in the countryside.*

Explanation: The highlighted section in the text shows that the answer is **C**, although words from the other two options (cities, countryside, car) are also mentioned.

Listening: Part 1 multiple choice

 TIP: In some questions, you will be asked to identify a speaker's opinion, attitude or feelings, so be sure to practise listening to texts where these are expressed.

Example

Here is a question from a Part 1 task about youth hostels, together with part of the tapescript.

 How does the woman feel about the future of youth hostels?

A worried by the way charges are increasing

B concerned about new activity schemes ✓

C upset at the proposed closures

TAPESCRIPT

MAN: What's all this about closing down some of the more remote hostels?

WOMAN: It's true – some are going to close, but they were under-used, so it makes economic sense. More of a problem for me is the 'Do it for real' initiative – some hostels are going to offer music and drama courses, rock climbing, football. I mean, is that what youth hostels are about? Charges are going up, of course, and nobody's entirely happy about that, but youth hostels still provide good value for money.

Explanation: The highlighted section of the text shows that B is the answer – that the woman feels concerned.

Listening: Part 2 sentence completion

 TIP: Read each sentence before you begin listening and think about the type of information that might fit the gap before you begin.

Examples

Here are some sentences from a Part 2 task, in which a conservationist called Sarah is talking about a type of insect called a glow-worm, together with the parts of the tapescript where you can find the answers.

> Sarah tells us about a teenager who thought several glow-worms on a ❶ ...... were in danger.

> I recently received a call from a teenager, who rang me in a state of alarm to say she was on a tennis court when she spotted half a dozen glow-worms on a footpath, and was worried they might get trampled on by players making their way to and from the court.

Explanation: You need to listen for a place where you might find a glow-worm. 'Trampled on' tells you that the glow-worms are in danger, so the correct answer is '**footpath**'.

> Sarah mentions the use of ❷ ...... as something which confuses male glow-worms.

> ... the males really seem to need darkness in order to see the females glowing, so we could consider reducing the numbers of street lights we have, which appear to disorient them.

Explanation: You need to listen for an object which confuses male glow-worms. 'Use of' suggests that this is probably not something natural in their environment, so the answer is '**street lights**'.

> *Remember that the words you write must be the exact words you hear on the recording.*

Listening: Part 2 sentence completion

 TIP: You may hear more than one possible word which you think could fill the gap.

Examples

Here are some sentences from a Part 2 task, in which a conservationist is talking about a type of insect called a glow-worm, together with the parts of the tapescript where you can find the answers.

> The time to look for the glow-worm in Europe is between May and ❶ ...September...

 In most parts of Europe, you'll have a good chance of seeing them if you go outside at dusk, beginning in May. They can be visible right up to September – although people often think they're only around up to the end of June or possibly July ...

Explanation: You can see from the sentence that the word to fill the gap is likely to be the name of a month. You hear the names of four months – May, June, July and September – in the text, but only one gives the answer.

> The glow-worm's diet consists of ❷ ...snails...

 People often ask what glow-worms eat, and assume it's going to be things like ants, flies or even leaves. They get a shock when they discover it's actually snails.

Explanation: From the sentence, we can guess that the word in the gap will be something that is edible to an insect. Several things are mentioned – ants, flies, leaves and snails – but snails are the things they eat. Sometimes locating the answer can depend on referencing, as in this example where 'they' refers to 'people' and 'it' refers to the thing glow-worms eat.

Listening: Part 3 multiple choice

 TIP: Look through the options before you listen. Use the first listening to select the most likely answer, and confirm your choice on the second listening.

Example

Here is a question from a Part 3 task, an interview with an Australian novelist called Herbie Otway, and the relevant part of the tapescript.

 What does Herbie tell us about his upbringing?

A His mother's pride in him gave him self-confidence. ✓

B He learnt a lot from his parents' balanced view of life.

C His father's support was crucial for Herbie's early writing.

D His parents saw the value of having a formal education.

 HERBIE:

TAPESCRIPT

Well, you know, my father was a car salesman, and he'd been a horse trader. So he knew all about the vast open spaces of the Australian outback and passed his know-how on to me. He was tough and smart, but if I showed him a poem I'd written, he'd say, 'Don't talk to me about that, go ask your mother.' She'd been, briefly, to a fancy school, so she was the one with the brains and education. I'd watch her telling her friends about my little achievements, just sort of glowing, she'd be, and that made me feel good about myself.

Explanation: **B**, **C** and **D** are incorrect because Herbie only mentions learning from his father's balanced view of life (B), his mother's support (C), and does not refer to his parents' opinions about formal education (D). The correct answer is therefore **A**. ✓

Listening: Part 3 multiple choice

 TIP: If you find it hard to get the answer to the question, try eliminating the options you know are wrong – and don't forget, you hear the recording twice.

Example

Here is a question from a Part 3 task, an interview with an Australian novelist called Herbie Otway, and the relevant part of the tapescript.

 Why did Herbie change from writing novels to writing short stories?

A He was disappointed by poor sales of his early novels.

B He was advised to try something less ambitious than novels. ✓

C He knew that short stories were in greater demand.

D He assumed short stories were of higher literary worth than novels.

TAPESCRIPT

INTERVIEWER: Now, why did you start your writing career with short stories? Isn't it more usual to kick off with a novel?

HERBIE: Strangely enough, I <u>didn't</u> start off writing short stories. I thought in my ignorance that a novel would be the thing to establish a name for myself in the literary world, so I wrote two. And when neither was accepted, it was my agent who told me to lower my sights and write a few stories. I only wrote the stories because I was sick of rejection, and writing a short story was a bit like building myself a nice solid shed that I knew wouldn't fall down. Later on, my publishers asked for more such stories, but I got my novels published first before writing more.

Explanation:

A is wrong because although he wrote two novels they were not accepted for publication.

C is wrong because he only wrote short stories as he was tired of being rejected.

D is wrong because he believed at the beginning that novels would establish his name as a writer, but admitted this was 'in my ignorance'.

The highlighted words in the tapescript show you that the correct answer is B. ✓

Listening: Part 4 multiple matching

 TIP: Read through both tasks. The words you hear will not be the same as the words in the tasks, but there will be key words and expressions that indicate the answer.

Example

Here is an example from a Part 4 task.

 You hear five extracts in which people are talking about their occupations.

statistician	cashier
accountant	news reporter
musician	careers advisor
librarian	fitness trainer

 SPEAKER 1

When I'm practising a piece, it's great, it gives me a real feeling of joy although I don't always get the notes right.

Explanation: The key words and expressions here are: **practising a piece** and **notes**. These indicate that the speaker is a musician.

 SPEAKER 2

... I do like clients to feel that they'd come back to me for business advice. I wouldn't want them to have someone else doing their books ...

Explanation: The key words and expressions are: **clients, business advice** and **doing their books**. These indicate that the speaker is an accountant.

NOTE: This is one of two matching tasks in Part 4.

Listening: Part 4 multiple matching

 TIP: In the texts you listen to, there will be information which may make more than one answer look attractive. Listen carefully to check your answers.

Example

Here is an example from a Part 4 task about happiness.

 Choose from the list what happiness involves for each speaker.

overcoming difficulties

appreciating ordinary things

not being under pressure of time

realising ambition

being generous

being an optimist

having a treat

liking other people

 SPEAKER 1

I think we have to learn what makes us, as individuals, happy. Some people have to have a special occasion or something unusual or uplifting, but those things aren't necessary for me … I just sit here and savour a good cup of coffee – that's what makes me happy.

Explanation: The speaker clearly says what makes him happy, but at the beginning he also refers to 'a special occasion'. This begins to make 'having a treat' seem attractive as an answer, but in fact the speaker is talking about 'some people', not himself. It's important to listen carefully.

NOTE: This is one of two matching tasks in Part 4.

 *Some candidates look at both tasks at the same time. Other candidates concentrate first on Task One and then, when the recording is repeated, on Task Two. Doing practice tests will show you which method is successful for you.*

General tips for Listening

1 Make sure you use the preparation time to read and listen to the instructions for each part so that you understand what you have to do.

2 Use the pause before each listening to read through all the questions and think about the type of answer that is required.

3 You hear the recordings twice, so use the second listening to check your answers even if you think they are correct.

4 In **Part 1**, remember not to choose your answer too soon, as the correct answer may come later in the listening.

5 In **Part 2**, remember to write the exact word(s) you hear and make sure you complete the sentence so it is grammatically correct.

6 In **Part 3**, remember to focus on the question stems so you can match the answer to the closest option when you listen.

7 Practise some **Part 4** tasks so you can see what method works best for you in approaching the task.

8 Remember that your final answer is the one you copy onto the answer sheet. Check that you have followed the numbering correctly. Remember that the answer needed will be a letter – A, B, C, etc. – for **Parts 1, 3** and **4** and a word, number or phrase for **Part 2**.

9 Don't leave a blank space on your answer sheet. If you're not sure of an answer, have a guess. You may have understood more than you think.

NOW YOU TRY! You will find a complete Listening paper to try on the CD-ROM, as well as all the recordings you need. Give yourself 40 minutes to work through the whole paper.

When you have finished you can check your answers.

Paper 5: Speaking

What's in the Speaking test?

Part 1 ⓠ conversation between the interlocutor and each candidate – a social exchange

Part 2 ⓠ you compare and speculate about 3 photographs and answer a question

Part 3 ⓠ you carry out a decision-making task with the other candidate and try to reach a decision

Part 4 ⓠ further discussion related to the task in Part 3

🕒 **15 minutes** *per pair of candidates*

Your speaking is assessed on:

- your accurate and appropriate use of a range of grammatical structures
- your use of a range of vocabulary
- your ability to link together what you say, without too much hesitation
- your pronunciation
- your ability to initiate and develop communication with your partner
- your overall effectiveness in dealing with the tasks.

Speaking: Part 1 interview

 TIP: The first part of the test is a general conversation between you and the interlocutor, so use it to relax and prepare yourself for the rest of the test. Try to link your points together and develop what you say.

Examples
Here are some questions and sample answers.

1

INTERLOCUTOR:	**What were the most useful things you learnt at school?**
CANDIDATE:	Well, obviously learning to read and count were really important – without those I couldn't have studied all the other subjects. On a social level I learnt how to get on with other people, and that was really valuable. In fact, it's helped me in the job I do now.

2

INTERLOCUTOR:	**What are the benefits of speaking another language?**
CANDIDATE:	Well, I'd say it's helped me to understand a bit more about how my own language works! I've found that because I can speak another language, I've been able to make friends with people from other countries. It's given me a greater understanding of other cultures, too.

3

INTERLOCUTOR:	**What do you think tourists would find interesting about your country?**
CANDIDATE:	There's a real mix of urban and rural life – you can enjoy the cities, or get far away from them to some very remote countryside. I think visitors also like the fact that people in my country are very hospitable – they always say they feel welcome there.

4

INTERLOCUTOR:	**How do you keep up with the news?**
CANDIDATE:	I don't buy a newspaper very often but I watch the news on TV when I can. I also look at different news websites, especially in my country, so I'm usually quite up to date with the news. I don't follow all the small details in the news, but I try to keep up with the bigger events - things going on around the world. Also, I try to read news magazines sometimes because the articles often go into more depth than what I see on TV.

Explanation: Each answer above gives at least two points in response to the question, with linkers and cohesive devices highlighted in the text.

Speaking: Part 2 long turn

 TIP: Make sure you give an extended answer to fill the 1 minute available and that you cover all the points.

Example

Here is an example of a Part 2 Speaking task and part of a sample answer. You can find the pictures for this task on page 56.

INTERLOCUTOR: **Here are your pictures. They show people taking part in different races.**

I'd like you to compare two of the pictures and say why the people might have decided to take part in the races, and what difficulties they might have during the race.

CANDIDATE:

COMPARE

Well, they're both pictures of people racing, but one shows a sailing race that looks as though it could be on the sea, whereas the other is an aerial view of a motor race, with a lot of spectators.

WHY TAKE PART

I think the competitors might have chosen to take part because they've found that they have a talent for that particular sport. Both sports require a lot of judgement and skill, though one is on land and the other is on water. Also, some people are simply addicted to the adrenaline rush they get from trying to win in these sports.

WHAT DIFFICULTIES

As for what difficulties they might have – well, both sports can be dependent on the weather, so that might give the competitors problems. You need a reasonable wind to be able to sail and you're almost bound to get soaking wet, and wet conditions can make motor racing even more hazardous than it already is. Mechanical failure might also be an issue during the motor race.

Explanation: The candidate's answer is good as it compares the two pictures and also addresses both the other points within the question.

Use the questions above the photos which the interlocutor gives you to remind you what you must talk about.

- Why might the people have decided to take part in the races?
- What difficulties might they have during the race?

Speaking: Part 2 long turn

 TIP: At the end of your partner's turn, you will be asked a question relating to the same set of pictures. You have up to 30 seconds to say what you think.

Example

Here is an example of a question which the listening candidate had to answer in Part 2. You can find the pictures on page 56.

INTERLOCUTOR:	**Which race do you think would be the most difficult to win and why?**
CANDIDATE:	I think the skating race might be the hardest, – there are so many people taking part, the chances of winning must be slim. And I imagine that unless you're very skilled it'd be extremely easy to fall over and then you'd be out of the race altogether.

Explanation: This is a good answer as it is short and to the point, but at the same time provides enough relevant language to cover the task.

Speaking: Part 3 collaborative task

 TIP: You have to work with another candidate for this part, so encourage your partner to join in the discussion too – don't try to do all the speaking yourself. Invite your partner to contribute if he/she is keeping quiet.

Example

In this example of a Part 3 task, you have to imagine that a company wants to improve working conditions for its employees. You have to discuss the changes the company is thinking of introducing and then choose two changes which would be the most popular. You can find the pictures on pages 60–61.

INTERLOCUTOR:	**First, talk to each other about what effect these changes might have on employees. Then decide which two changes would be the most popular.**
CANDIDATE A:	So what do you think about the first picture?
CANDIDATE B:	Well, if the company introduced a gym or an exercise class like the picture in the top right, it would mean that staff wouldn't have to go elsewhere to get their exercise.
CANDIDATE A:	They could easily go after work, so they could use their time more effectively. And, who knows, a fitter workforce might be a more productive one. What do you think?
CANDIDATE B:	Hmm, that's true, but …
CANDIDATE A:	Yes, that's right. And I suppose …

Explanation: The first candidate invites their partner to give an opinion and, after agreeing, expands on the idea. Intonation can also be used to encourage your partner to agree or disagree.

Speaking: **Part 3** collaborative task

 TIP: You need to interact with your partner, make suggestions and express opinions, and respond to what your partner says.

Example

In this example of a Part 3 task, you have to imagine that a company wants to improve working conditions for its employees. You have to discuss the changes it is thinking of introducing and then choose two changes which would be the most popular. You can find the pictures on pages 60–61.

CANDIDATE A: I guess it's a workplace nursery for children. That'd be pretty popular in my opinion – you'd be near your kids and you wouldn't have to spend time driving to a nursery before you went to work. D'you agree?

CANDIDATE B: Absolutely – it'd certainly be popular, though perhaps the staff would prefer to have a really comfortable staffroom – where they could get away from their desks for a bit. Not many companies have those, do they?

CANDIDATE A: No. You're right. And what about …?

Explanation: The candidates interact well with each other, using language of agreement, opinion and inviting comment, as shown in the highlighted words.

 *Remember to answer both the questions printed above the pictures which the interlocutor gives you and not to make your final decision until you have talked about most of the pictures.*

- What effect might these changes have on employees?
- Which two changes would be the most popular?

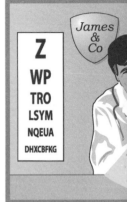

Speaking: **Part 4** discussion

 TIP: You will be asked to give your opinion in Part 4. These phrases may help you:

Giving your opinion

In my view ...

As far as I'm concerned ...

If you ask me ...

To be honest, I think ...

Generally speaking, I'd say ...

That's a difficult question ...

I'm not sure what I think about that ...

I have mixed views on that ...

Agreeing and disagreeing

Absolutely.

I couldn't agree more.

I'd go along with that.

I think you're right.

I'm afraid I don't agree.

Yes, but on the other hand ...

I don't think that's always true, but ...

 *Always say something, and give an opinion! It doesn't matter if it's right or wrong – you are being assessed on your language, not your ideas, and the examiners want to hear your full range of language.*

General tips for Speaking

1 Make sure you speak loudly and clearly enough for both examiners to hear you during the test.

2 Try to use a wide range of grammar and vocabulary during the test. The examiners can only award you marks for the language you produce.

3 Try to keep talking in the different parts until the interlocutor says 'Thank you.'

4 Don't worry if the interlocutor stops you before you have said everything you want to. The test is carefully timed and it is important to keep to the timings. You will be given the exact time specified in the test.

5 Ask for repetition if you are uncertain about what to do.

6 For **Part 2** practise talking alone for 1 minute about a selection of photos: speculate about the photos – don't just describe them.

7 For **Part 3** practise working with a partner: discuss different pictures, expressing ideas and giving opinions.

8 Remember that you are being assessed on your language and not your ideas.

9 Try to relax and enjoy the test!

 NOW YOU TRY! You will find a video of a complete Speaking test to try on the CD-ROM, together with the pictures and the script for the interlocutor. Practise with a partner, and you will feel more confident when you take the test.

What to do on the day

Very few people like taking exams, but you can make the day of the exam easier if you make sure you know what to expect and what you will have to do before you go to the exam centre or place where you take your CAE exam.

Rules and regulations

For any exam you take, there are some rules and regulations about what you **must** do and what you **mustn't** do during the exam. Read through the Cambridge ESOL rules and regulations below and if there is anything you don't understand, ask your teacher. On the day of the exam, you can also ask the examination supervisor if you are not sure.

You must ...

- provide a valid photographic proof of your identity (for example: national identity card, passport, college ID or driving licence) and your Statement of Entry for each paper you take.
- only have on your desk what you need to complete the examination (pens, pencils and erasers).
- switch off your mobile phone and any other electronic device. The supervisor will tell you where you have to put them.
- stop writing immediately when you are told to do so.

You must not ...

- cheat, copy, give anything to another candidate, take anything from another candidate, or break any of the rules during the examination.
- use, or attempt to use, a dictionary.
- use correction fluid on the answer sheets.
- talk to or disturb other candidates during the examination.
- smoke or eat in the examination room. However, you are allowed to drink plain, still water from a plastic bottle with a secure lid.

Advice and information

We hope that all our candidates will have a positive experience of taking a Cambridge ESOL exam. So, we have prepared some advice and information so that you know what to do if there are any problems on the day that you take your exam. Make sure that you have read and understood all the information and advice below before you go into the exam.

Make sure you are on time

- Know the date, time and place of your examination and arrive well before the start time.
- If you arrive late for any part of the examination, report to the supervisor or invigilator. You may not be allowed to take the examination. Also, if you are admitted, not all of your work may be accepted.
- If you miss any part of the examination, you will not normally be given a grade.

Instructions for taking the test

- The supervisor will tell you what you have to do. The instructions are also written on the question paper and the answer sheet.
- Listen to the supervisor and read the instructions carefully.
- Tell the supervisor or invigilator at once if you think you have the wrong question paper, or if the question paper is incomplete or badly printed.
- See page 68 if you are taking Computer-based CAE (CB CAE).

Advice and assistance during the examination

- If you are not sure about what to do, raise your hand to attract attention. The invigilator will come to help you.
- You must not ask for, and will not be given, any explanation of the questions.
- If you do not feel well on the day of the examination or think that your work may be affected for any other reason, tell the supervisor or invigilator.

Leaving the examination room

- Do not leave the examination room for any reason without the permission of the supervisor or invigilator.
- The supervisor will tell you when you can and can't leave the room.
- You must wait until the supervisor has collected your question paper, answer sheet(s) and any paper used for rough work before you leave the examination room.
- You must not take any information relating to the examination questions or answers out of the examination room.
- Do not make any noise near the examination room.

Answer sheets (for the paper and pencil test)

On the day you take the exam, you can write on the question paper while you decide what the correct answer is. However, when you have made a decision, you **must** transfer your final answers onto the candidate answer sheets which the supervisor will give you for the Reading, Use of English and Listening papers.

How to complete the answer sheets

You can see an example of what an answer sheet looks like on page 67. There are instructions on the answer sheets to tell you how you should fill them in, but here are the main things you need to know:

- It is very important that you use a pencil to write your answers on the answer sheets. (We use a special machine to check some of your answers and it can only 'see' pencil marks.)
- Where you have to choose an answer (A, B, C or D, etc.), you must make a clear pencil mark inside the box you choose. Don't, for example, put a circle around the box, because the machine won't 'see' this.
- If you have to write a word or phrase for your answer, please write clearly. If the examiners can't read your writing, they won't know if your answer is correct or not.
- If you change your mind about an answer, it is important that you use an eraser to rub out the answer you don't want.

CAE Paper 1 Reading Candidate Answer Sheet

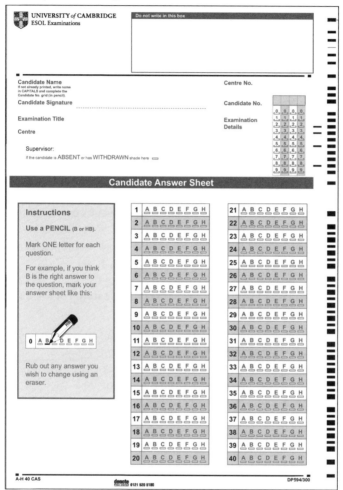

Paper 2 Writing

You write your answers for the Writing paper on the paper itself, not on an answer sheet. You must write your answers in **pen** not pencil. You can cross out any mistakes you make, but you need to make sure your writing is clear for the examiner.

If you are taking CB CAE you type your answers on the screen and there is a word counter to help you.

Computer-based CAE (CB CAE)

There is a computer-based exam for CAE that leads to the internationally recognised Cambridge ESOL certificate. This computer version of CAE is available to centres with the appropriate equipment and training. The tasks are exactly the same as for the paper and pencil test. The only thing that is different is that you take the Reading, Writing, Use of English and Listening papers on a computer.

If you prefer to take the test on a computer there are other aspects of CB CAE that may be an advantage:

- You can take CB CAE at a range of different times in the year.
- You can register for the exam as little as two weeks before taking it.
- Your results are available online just three weeks after you take the test.

When you are taking the exam, there are certain features of the CB test that will help you:

- There is a tutorial that you can watch before taking the test, which gives you advice on how to complete your answers.
- You can edit your answers on screen during the exam, so if you decide to change something it is easy to do so.
- There is a clock on screen which shows you how much time you have left.
- On the Reading paper you can scroll through the longer texts. You can also go backwards and forwards through the sections. This means you can read part of a text again if you want to check something.
- You write your answers on screen for the Writing paper. There is a word counter, which shows you how many words you have written.
- You are able to use headphones during the Listening paper, so you adjust the volume if you need to.
- Remember that the Speaking paper for CB CAE is carried out in the same way as the paper and pencil exam.

If you are interested in doing CB CAE, you should contact your exam centre to find out more.

NOTE: The CAE exam on the *Top Tips for CAE* CD-ROM looks like a CB CAE exam, but the real CB CAE exam does not include all the same features.

What next after CAE?

We hope that you will enjoy studying for CAE and that you will be successful when you take the exam. A Cambridge ESOL qualification is a great achievement and you can be proud of your result.

When you receive your results and certificate, you will probably start to think about what you can do next to continue to improve your English, so here are some suggestions:

Using CAE for work or study

All around the world, CAE is a well-respected Cambridge ESOL examination. Many companies and educational institutions in different countries recognise CAE as proof of your level of English when you are looking for a job or applying for a place to study.

For the future, you may be thinking about studying abroad or working in a company where you need to use your English. If this is something which interests you, have a look at the Recognition database on the Cambridge ESOL website:

www.CambridgeESOL.org/recognition

Search the database for the specific information you need about how and where you can use CAE. Using the information in the database, you can find out about the many possibilities, both for work and further study, which are open to you when you pass CAE.

Taking the next Cambridge ESOL exam

If you are thinking of continuing your English studies, the next level of the Cambridge ESOL exams for you is the Certificate of Proficiency in English (CPE). You can find more information about CPE on our Candidate Support website at:

www.candidates.CambridgeESOL.org

Installing the *Top Tips for CAE* CD-ROM

Please set your screen resolution to 800 x 600 to get the best out of your *Top Tips for CAE* CD-ROM.

For Microsoft Windows

1 Insert the *Top Tips for CAE* CD-ROM into your CD-ROM drive. If you have Autorun enabled, Windows will automatically launch the Installation wizard for installing *Top Tips for CAE*. If not, double click the Top_Tips_for CAE.exe from the CD-ROM.
2 Follow the Installation wizard steps.
3 After the installation completes, you can access the application from the Start menu.
4 You can also launch the application by double clicking the shortcut on the Desktop.
5 To uninstall the application, click Uninstall Top Tips for CAE from the Start menu.

For Mac OS X (10.3 or later)

Top Tips for CAE is distributed as a package ('.pkg') file for Mac OS X:

1 Insert the *Top Tips for CAE* CD-ROM into your CD-ROM drive. The *Top Tips for CAE* icon will appear on your Desktop.
2 Double click the icon. Mac OS X will display the contents of the CD-ROM.
3 Double click the file 'Top Tips for CAE.pkg'. This will launch the installer.
4 Simply click continue on the Installer's Welcome screen to proceed with the installation.
5 Just before the Installer copies the files, you will need to enter the administrator's password.
6 After the installation is completed, the Top Tips for CAE application will reside as a folder named *Top Tips for CAE* inside the applications folder.
7 Double click the Top tips for CAE folder to view its contents.
8 Then double click the Top Tips for CAE file to launch *Top Tips for CAE*.

9 NOTE: To easily open *Top Tips for CAE*, you can drag it to the dock.
10 To uninstall the application move the Top Tips for CAE folder from the Applications folder to the Trash.

System requirements

For PC

Essential:	Windows 2000, XP or Vista, CD drive & audio capabilities
Recommended:	400 MHz processor or faster, with 256mb of RAM or more

For Mac

Essential:	Mac OS X, version 10.3 or higher
Recommended:	400 MHz G3 processor or faster, with 256mb of RAM or more